# WHERE *Heaven* MEETS *You*

A Message for Women

VIRGINIA H. PEARCE

SALT LAKE CITY, UTAH

Visit us at DeseretBook.com

ISBN 978-1-62972-188-0

Printed in the United States of America
Artistic Printing, Salt Lake City, UT

10 9 8 7 6 5 4 3 2 1

I will never forget my first experience in an impoverished country. It was a Church assignment, and there were many things that were new to me. As we drove from the airport to our lodgings, we passed huge heaps of smoking garbage, glimpsing people who were scavenging in the refuse for things to sell. We saw families in tents by the side of the road and children begging at car windows whenever traffic slowed. I watched, smelled, listened, trying to make sense of it all. But the memory that is etched in my heart more than any other from that visit was of an afternoon on a small island. We climbed out of the ferry and walked down a wide dusty road. Mangy dogs, pigs, and beautiful children followed us until we came to our destination. Walking over wooden planks and ducking our heads, we entered the home of a family. Two small rooms. The walls were louvered slats, through which the children from the village watched us curiously. Limited by language, we couldn't communicate verbally. The family sang Primary songs. We joined in. We prayed together, hugged, and parted. I didn't quite know what to say as we left the island. I felt I should express horror and sadness over the distressing circumstances in which these people lived. But, I couldn't—in fact, I felt a bit envious. I didn't really understand then, but I think I do now.

Sister Rosemary Wixom, general Primary president, spoke at a CES fireside at Utah State University of very different circumstances, but in a way that gave words to the feelings I had on that long-ago day in the Philippines. Sister Wixom recounted one of *her* memories: "It was a beautiful fall day as we loaded up the family car with all of our belongings. You see, I was off to college with my twin sister, and our mother was going to drive us and drop us off in Logan [Utah]. . . . We were excited. We had every piece of clothing and every shoe we owned, plus food to stock our cupboards, packed into that car. We could barely see out the windows. As we drove into this valley, I had butterflies in my stomach. I could hardly wait for the adventure ahead.

"On campus one could feel the excitement in the air as students were unloading their cars and moving their belongings into their dorms and apartments. . . .

"When the car was empty, we stood on the sidewalk . . . , holding the last few items from the backseat. There we were, with jars of bottled peaches in our arms as we waved good-bye to our mother. Then, as she drove away, reality hit. We turned to each other, and with tears running down our cheeks, we said: 'What have we done? What were we thinking? How could something we once thought to be so adventurous now seem so frightening and intimidating?' Little did I know that in the days and years ahead on this campus, I would make decisions that would define the rest of my life. It was here [in Logan] that I discovered I had my own beliefs, and I was faced with defending my faith. I made lifelong friends. My prayers became more sincere. My testimony began to grow. I learned it was a personal choice to stand up for my standards and stretch myself academically and spiritually.

". . . No wonder this Cache Valley, this university, this campus is so beautiful to me. For it was here that I would begin to come to know myself, and in the process of coming to know myself, I would begin to come to know the Savior."[1]

Thinking back to that little home on a dusty island, it is no wonder that it seemed so beautiful to me. Within those flimsy walls, that family had come to know God. And for those few minutes we spent with them, we all shared heavenly light.

It is individual and collective experiences between God and His children that unite us and turn ordinary places into sacred places.

That is exactly what happened to those who listened to Alma at the Waters of Mormon. Fleeing from King Noah, Alma hid during the day in a thicket of trees in the borders of the land. Many who believed his words came to be taught. Gathering in tents with their families in "a place which was called Mormon" (Mosiah 18:4), they listened eagerly as Alma taught the gospel of Jesus Christ. And then, going into the waters of Mormon, they covenanted with God to serve him and keep his commandments. Baptizing Helam, the first of many, Alma "cried, saying: O Lord, pour out thy Spirit upon thy servant, that he may do this work with holiness of heart" (Mosiah 18:12).

"And now it came to pass that all this was done in Mormon, yea, by the waters of Mormon, . . . the forest of Mormon, how beautiful are they to the eyes of them who there came to the knowledge of their Redeemer; yea, and how blessed are they, for they shall sing to his praise forever" (Mosiah 18:30).

The Waters of Mormon was a place made beautiful and sacred through holy experiences.

Elder Marlin K. Jensen taught: "There are places on this earth that have been made sacred by what happened there. According to the Old Testament, one of these places is Sinai, Horeb, or 'the mountain of God' (Exodus 3:1; see also Exodus 3:12; 34:2), where the Lord appeared to Moses in the burning bush. As Moses approached the bush, the Lord said to him, 'Draw not nigh hither: put off thy shoes from off thy feet, for the place whereon thou standest is holy ground (Exodus 3:5).'"[2]

The Garden of Gethsemane; the shores of Galilee; the Sacred Grove; the John Johnson home in Hyrum, Ohio; the upper floor of the Red Brick Store in Nauvoo—

because of what happened between God and men and women in these places, they are holy.

There is a Celtic expression, "thin places." A thin place is where the veil that separates heaven and earth is nearly transparent. It is a place where we experience a deep sense of God's presence in our everyday world. A thin place is where, for a moment, the spiritual world and the natural world intersect.

> *"Thin places," the Celts call this space,*
> *Both seen and unseen,*
> *Where the door between this world*
> *And the next is cracked open for a moment*
> *And the light is not all on the other side.*
> *God shaped space. Holy.*[3]

Certainly temples are "thin places." Think about that. Above the entrance to each temple the words "Holiness to the Lord" are written. We call a temple the House of the Lord. Certainly, it is God-shaped space.

I have had the unearned privilege of walking through newly finished temples the evening before dedicatory services as our leaders inspected the workmanship of the building itself—the finishings and furnishings, the paintings, the grounds, crafted and installed as a form of worship. After many months, even years, of skilled work, it all comes together on the day of dedication—a space that is peaceful, clean, orderly, and beautiful. Looking at the workmanship and materials, President Hinckley would usually say, "Nothing is too good for the Lord."

Temples are refuges in a world full of noise, fear, and sleaze. We dress appropriately, speak quietly, and enter with hearts turned toward our Creator and Redeemer. We bring our perplexities, our sorrows, our yearnings, and our joy into those sacred buildings. We come as our true selves, unadorned by position or distinctive dress. We come knowing that God accepts us in our imperfections and knows how much we desire—in spite of our weakness—to be like Him. We receive comfort, revelation, and love. We solemnly and gratefully accept the ordinances—within which lie the power of godliness. After all, it is in temples that we are endowed with His greatest gift—His unfathomable power. Herein lies the sacredness of temples.

But let me remind you of another building—one so different in construction, appointments, and purpose. A small, rough-hewn, impregnable prison in Clay County, Missouri. We know it as Liberty Jail. Joseph Smith and five other leaders were incarcerated there during the winter of 1838 through 1839—the coldest winter on record in the state of Missouri. It was a grim place, with only one small, heavy door on the main floor opening to the outside world. The dungeon on the lower floor was barely six feet high—floor to ceiling—making it impossible for Joseph to stand straight. Bare rough stones formed the floor, covered with a bit of loose, dirty straw. I quote from Elder Jeffrey R. Holland, as he describes that winter:

"The food given to the prisoners was coarse and sometimes contaminated, so filthy that one of them said they 'could not eat it until [they] were driven to it by hunger.' On as many as four occasions poison was administered to them in their food, making them so violently ill that for days they alternated between vomiting and a kind of delirium, not really caring whether they lived or died.

"In the Prophet Joseph's letters, he spoke of the jail being a 'hell, surrounded with demons . . . where we are compelled to hear nothing but blasphemous oaths, and witness a scene of blasphemy, and drunkenness and hypocrisy, and debaucheries of every description.' 'We have . . . not blankets sufficient to keep us warm; and when we have a fire, we are obliged to have almost a constant smoke.' 'Our souls have been bowed down' and 'my nerve trembles from long confinement,' Joseph wrote. 'Pen, or tongue, or angels,' could not adequately describe 'the malice of hell' that he suffered there."[4]

With all of that, B. H. Roberts referred to Liberty Jail as a "prison-temple."[5] What could he have meant? Certainly, the purposes of a prison are the exact antithesis of the purposes of a temple—one is to incarcerate, hold captive, punish. The other is to set free, to give power, to glorify.

And yet, as I think of those Celtic "thin places" I say, oh yes! Liberty Jail was a place where Joseph's very suffering and despondency made him ready to receive God. Desperately, he begged for help. The answer came. "My son, peace be unto thy soul" (D&C 121:7). "God shall give unto you knowledge by his Holy Spirit, yea, by the unspeakable gift of the Holy Ghost. . . . Nothing shall be withheld. . . . All thrones and dominions, principalities and powers, shall be revealed and set forth upon all who have endured valiantly for the gospel of Jesus Christ" (D&C 121:26, 28–29). Joseph was told that "the doctrine of the priesthood shall distill upon thy soul as the dews from heaven. The Holy Ghost shall be thy constant companion, and thy scepter an unchanging scepter of righteousness and truth; and thy dominion shall be an everlasting dominion, and without compulsory means it shall flow unto thee forever and ever" (D&C 121:45–46). Liberty Jail had become sacred space, a thin place,

*Where the door between this world*
*And the next was cracked open for a moment*
*And the light was not all on the other side.*[6]

Joseph left that prison-temple forever changed with increased moral strength and a greater capacity to influence for good.

A mother hummingbird builds a new home. She must create a place of physical safety and warmth, where she can give birth to, care for, and then launch her wee ones into the world.

Finding bits of fluff, soft plant matter, twigs, straw, and leaves, she weaves, pokes, and tamps them into shape. Adding spider webs to give the nest strength and flexibility, she works patiently, diligently. Back and forth, hither and yon, each nest is its own individual creation, made up of unique materials but perfectly, perfectly serviceable.

This little cup will securely hold her tiny eggs as she seals the opening with her own warmth—her life force. Is this pure instinct? I think so.

Like our busy little friend, we mothers prepare for our babies. We instinctively want a home that can physically lock out intruders. One where we can be warm when winter storms rage. One with a roof to shelter us from scorching sun.

But you and I are more purposeful than a hummingbird. You see, we desire more than physical safety. We add to basic instinct a God-given desire for the spiritual safety of our loved ones. We want a place where we can teach them, watch them grow in confidence and skill. We want them to know how to build loving and satisfying relationships. We want them to be prepared to contribute to the world, to be strong in the face of evil and adversity, to make and keep sacred covenants, and to ultimately be prepared to go back to their eternal home. And we know that as we teach them, we will also learn and grow.

Yes, we want our homes to be "thin places" where we, and all those who enter, can experience God.

We are taught that "only the home can compare with the temple in sacredness."[7]

What does that look like? Surely it doesn't mean a building with the finest appointments and workmanship. A place of complete order where people speak only in hushed tones, with light colored carpet and occasionally some soft organ music?

Wouldn't that be lovely! But in truth, our homes often resemble busy airports with people constantly coming and going. There seems to be an abundance of "stuff" that grows on every surface and spills onto floors. In these home-temples we laugh and cry together, experience anger and frustration as well as deep and spoken love. In our homes we sustain hurt and pain, make mistakes, learn, repent, forgive, change. Home is a refuge, but it is also a laboratory, a classroom. But in all this confusion we sense something grand. Isn't growing toward Godhood holy work? No wonder our homes are second only to temples in their sacredness.

Sadly enough, we have all been in homes that are dark, depressing, and chaotic. I'm not talking about the chaos of clutter. I am talking about the chaos and darkness that come from spiritual darkness—places large and small into which the Spirit of the Lord has not been invited.

Think about your home. Is it a place where every individual is safe to be himself—to cry, to be vulnerable and tired? Is it a place where there is an underlying atmosphere of love, making it easier to grow and learn and repent and contribute? Most of all, is it a place where you can be personally involved with God—where angels minister? Is it a thin place?

If these are your desires, you may want to consider dedicating your home or your apartment if you have not done so. It is a sweet thing to dedicate a home—to give voice to our commitment to do all we can to create a space where the Spirit of the Lord can dwell. If you have not dedicated your home and would like to do so, you may find informative help in *Handbook 2*, section 20.11.[8]

You may live in a home where a spouse or children or other occupants don't share your desire that it be a sacred place. What does that mean for you? Think back again to Liberty Jail. Nothing and no one can prevent us, as individual women, from having experiences with God. We can pray any time in any environment. We can feast on the scriptures. He can fill us with His love and power anywhere, anytime. Perhaps there may even be a particular place—a corner of a bedroom or a closet—where you go when you are filled with a desire to worship and supplicate your Father in Heaven—a space and place that is yours alone.

Teaching about the relationship between temples and homes, Elder John A. Widstoe wrote, "Spiritual power is generated within temple walls, and sent out to bless the world. Light from the house of the Lord illumines every home within the Church fitted for its reception by participation in temple privileges. Every home penetrated by the temple spirit enlightens, cheers, and comforts every member of the household. The peace we covet is found in such homes."[9] President Marion G. Romney said, "The power emanating from temples is far greater than we realize."[10]

So, if women are, by nature, a moral force for good in the world, think of that innate moral power when it is added upon through the temple endowment of power.

If we are faithful to the covenants we make with God

in His holy house, we literally bring His priesthood power into our environments—most particularly our homes. Joseph Smith, speaking to women, said, "If you live up to your privilege, the angels cannot be restrain'd from being your associates."[11] Angels for associates? Why would any of us fail to claim that privilege?

A little over four years ago, I found myself returning home from the funeral of my husband. My children and friends who had gathered and been ever-present during the days since his death had left reluctantly—"Do you want one of us to stay? It wouldn't be a problem. . . . Just for the night?"

"No," I said. "I'm okay." And so they left.

The door closed and I turned around, thinking of my new life ahead. I would be alone in this space that I had always shared with others. It was indeed quiet. Very quiet. And a wall of loneliness almost flattened me. But surprisingly, and at the same time, it felt oh-so-good. Rather than just a lonely empty house, I had been blessed with space that was holy where the door between this world and the next had cracked open many, many times. I thought with gratitude of the blessings of the covenants I had made—the companionship of the Holy Ghost and temple covenants that had given me access to God's priesthood power. Power that I now felt filling every corner.

During the next few weeks, I found it difficult to be away from my home for more than a few hours at a time. I'm sure some of that was due to the fatigue of grieving, but I believe that it was, in part, a new and deep recognition of the sacredness of home. Finding the notes I had written when my husband dedicated our home decades earlier, I was reminded that he had invited the Lord to watch over and protect and bless our home. And He had done so—and continues to do so.

Light is light. It doesn't come with the price of the neighborhood or the square footage of the house. And God's light doesn't stay in those thin places—it flows into our souls. We assimilate it and take it with us. Yes, the place and space is sacred, but more sacred are we—the vessels who carry his power.

A thirteen-year-old boy said to his mother: "I love you, Mom! When I'm with you it's like I'm inside a bubble—it's just so safe and happy." Getting out of the car on another morning, he said, "Here I go, leaving your bubble." His mother said, "Oh, no, my boy, you can take the bubble with you wherever you go!"

This is what we women do. We go to our Father in Heaven. Sometimes in sheer gratitude. Sometimes in discouragement or even desperation. We study His word. We do His will. We seek and accept the blessings of the temple where He endows us with His power and life-giving light. We are faithful to our covenants and we *expect* experiences with Him and His angels.

Hallowed by those experiences, our homes become "thin places" and we, ourselves, become a safe and happy home for others wherever we go.

## Notes


1. Rosemary M. Wixom, "Coming to Know," Church Educational System fireside for Young Adults, Utah State University, 1 May 2011; available at https://www.lds.org/broadcasts/article/print/ces-devotionals/2011/01/coming-to-know?lang=eng; accessed 7 July 2014.
2. Marlin K. Jensen, "Stand in the Sacred Grove," Church Educational System devotional for Young Adults, Sacramento, California, 6 May 2012; available at https://www.lds.org/broadcasts/article/print/ces-devotionals/2012/01/stand-in-the-sacred-grove?lang=eng&clang=eng; accessed 7 July 2014.
3. Sharlanda Sledge, unpublished poem, n.d.
4. Jeffrey R. Holland, "Lessons from Liberty Jail," *Ensign*, September 2009, 27–28.
5. See B. H. Roberts, *A Comprehensive History of the Church of Jesus Christ of Latter-day Saints*, 6 vols. (Salt Lake City: The Church of Jesus Christ of Latter-day Saints, 1930), 1:521 (chapter heading); see also 1:526.
6. Sharlanda Sledge, unpublished poem, n.d.
7. Bible Dictionary, s.v. "Temple," 780–81.
8. See *Handbook 2: Administering the Church* (Salt Lake City: The Church of Jesus Christ of Latter-day Saints, 2010), 176–77; available at https://www.lds.org/bc/content/shared/content/english/pdf/language-materials/08702_eng.pdf?lang=eng; accessed 8 July 2014.
9. John A. Widtsoe, "The House of the Lord," *Improvement Era* 39 (April 1936): 228.
10. Marion G. Romney, *Look to God and Live: Discourses of Marion G. Romney*, compiled by George J. Romney (Salt Lake City: Deseret Book, 1971), 236.
11. Relief Society Minute Book, 17 March 1842–16 March 1844, 35; available at http://josephsmithpapers.org/paperSummary/nauvoo-relief-society-minute-book?p=35; accessed 8 July 2014.